Intro

Dear Mom and Daughter,
Welcome to the "Threads of Love: A Mother-Daughter Journal!"

I salute your intention to deepen your mother-daughter bond and share, explore and communicate your uniqueness. I'm honoured to be part of that journey by providing you with the questions and prompts to support you with that.

The point of this journal is to allow you to dive deeper into your own personality and individuality while allowing you to explore the individuality and personality of the other. This is done with the help of expert-based questions, prompts, directions and exercises.

The questions are written in a form as if one of you asks the other, so when you read "me" imagine it is your daughter/mom asking the question.

Each page is named either
"Dear Daughter" or "Dear Mom" to help you
both have a respective page to write on. Plus,
each chapter end has two "Nothing Left Unsaid"
pages, where you can continue writing if you run out
of space, or add something that you want.

This journal will ask you to write, draw, color,
communicate, listen, and collaborate. This will ensure
that not only the outcome, but the sole journey of
filling out a journal together will be an activity that
will become a memory for years to come!

With that said - this journal has only one
requirement - Be open, honest, understanding, and
creative! Answer the questions and have fun sharing
them with one another!

Aside from the content, feel free to color the page
background and further personalize the journal.

Without further ado, I wish you a wonderful bonding
time while you explore the Threads of love!

With respect,
Mia Richard

Table of Contents

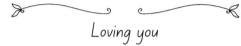

Chapter I - Our Unique Journey

Loving you
Hobbies
Feeling proud
Tradition for years to come
Our Family Tree
Nothing left unsaid

Chapter II - Letters to each other

Letter of gratitude
Letter of apology
Letter of strength
Letter of family love
Nothing left unsaid

Chapter III - Memories and Milestones

Special family moments
Who's the best at...
Funny mishaps
Being part of this
Our words
Nothing left unsaid

Chapter VII - Cooking and Baking Memories

My favorite recipe
Our favorite recipe
My favorite sweet
Our favorite sweet
What do we eat?
Go-to foods
Food traditions
Nothing left unsaid

Chapter VIII - Book and Movie Clubs

My favorite books list
You should read...
My favorite movie
You should watch...
Our favorite movie
Nothing left unsaid

Chapter IX - Travel and Adventure

Cherished memory of a family trip
Cherished memory of a solo trip
Going prepared
The perfect vacation
Nothing left unsaid

Chapter 1
Our Unique Journey

This chapter focuses on your own unique journey as a mother and daughter. This bond and relationship is one of a kind, completely different from any other mother-daughter relationship in the world.

During this chapter, you will have the chance to talk about your individual personality traits and joint activities as a mom and daughter and as a family. You will also dedicate some time and effort to your lineage and traditions, exploring what makes you - you.

I wish you love and feelings of appreciation, care and honor while exploring the threads of your unique journey together.

Dear Daughter,
Loving you...

What do you love and admire most about me?

What makes me unique?

What are my biggest strengths?

Dear Mom,
Loving you...

What do you love and admire most about me?

What makes me unique?

What are my biggest strengths?

Dear Daughter,
Hobbies we could do...

What is a hobby or a fun activity that we could do together?

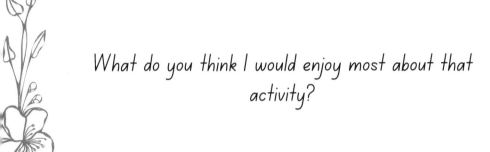

What do you think I would enjoy most about that activity?

What do we need to make this activity possible?

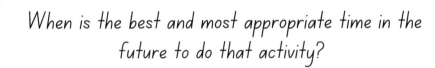

When is the best and most appropriate time in the future to do that activity?

Dear Mom,
Hobbies we could do...

✻

What is a hobby or a fun activity that we could do together?

What do you think I would enjoy most about that activity?

What do we need to make this activity possible?

When is the best and most appropriate time in the future to do that activity?

Dear Daughter,
Feeling proud of our family...

What is something that we as a family have achieved and you are proud of?

Why is that experience so special for you?

Dear Mom,
Feeling proud of our family...

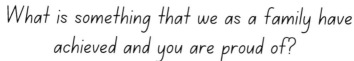

What is something that we as a family have achieved and you are proud of?

Why is that experience so special for you?

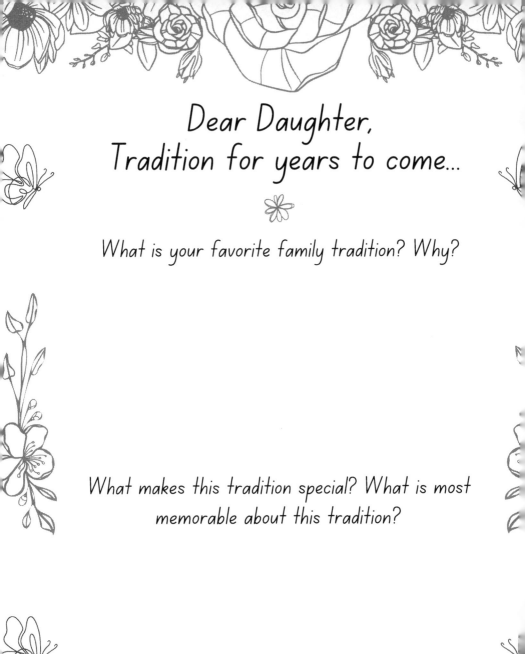

Dear Daughter,
Tradition for years to come...

What is your favorite family tradition? Why?

What makes this tradition special? What is most memorable about this tradition?

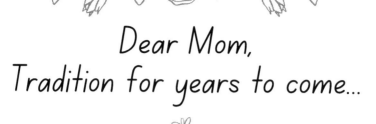

Dear Mom,
Tradition for years to come...

What is your favorite family tradition? Why?

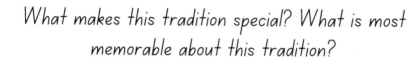

What makes this tradition special? What is most
memorable about this tradition?

Dear Mom and Daughter,
Our Family Tree...

✳

Make a family tree starting with the mother's parents.

*To have more width, you can turn the page horizontally.

Dear Daughter,
Nothing Left Unsaid...

On this page, write anything that you might have wanted to say but didn't get the chance to during this chapter about our Unique Journey.

Dear Mom,
Nothing Left Unsaid...

On this page, write anything that you might have wanted to say but didn't get the chance to during this chapter about our Unique Journey.

Chapter II
Letters to each other

The second chapter of this journal is dedicated to writing letters to one another, and to your family. Through writing, we can express ourselves in a creative, unique way, while also sharing what lies within our hearts.

In this chapter, you will have the chance to write letters to your mom/daughter/family on different topics, emotions, and values.

This chapter is all about expressing love, gratitude, strength, and forgiveness, so when you write or share your letters, try your best to feel these emotions in your heart.

Dear Daughter,
Letter of Gratitude

Write a letter to me in which you thank me for something I have done for you, which was very helpful. Explain the situation and why it is important for you, and express gratitude for my help.

Dear Mom,
Letter of Gratitude

Write a letter to me in which you thank me for something I have done for you, which was very helpful. Explain the situation and why it is important for you, and express gratitude for my help.

Dear Daughter,
Letter of Apology

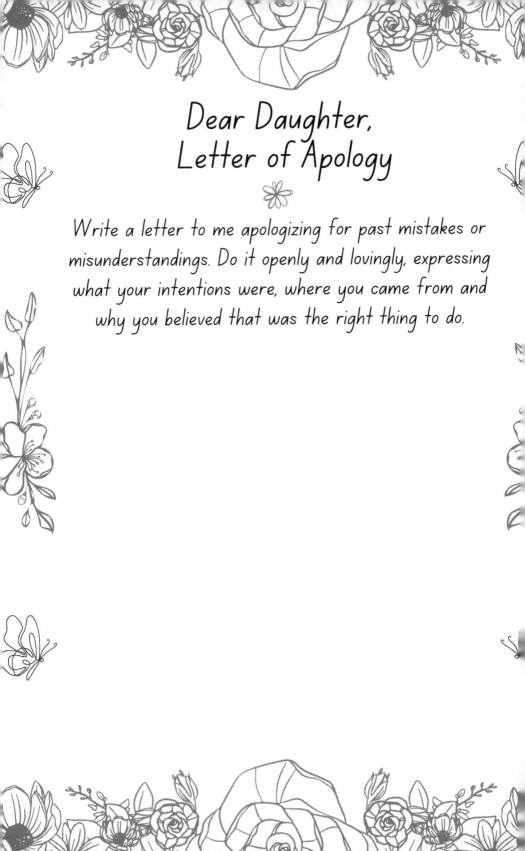

Write a letter to me apologizing for past mistakes or misunderstandings. Do it openly and lovingly, expressing what your intentions were, where you came from and why you believed that was the right thing to do.

Dear Mom,
Letter of Apology

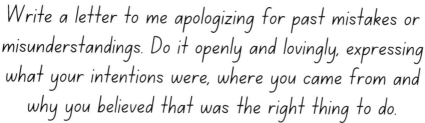

Write a letter to me apologizing for past mistakes or misunderstandings. Do it openly and lovingly, expressing what your intentions were, where you came from and why you believed that was the right thing to do.

Dear Daughter,
Letter of Strength

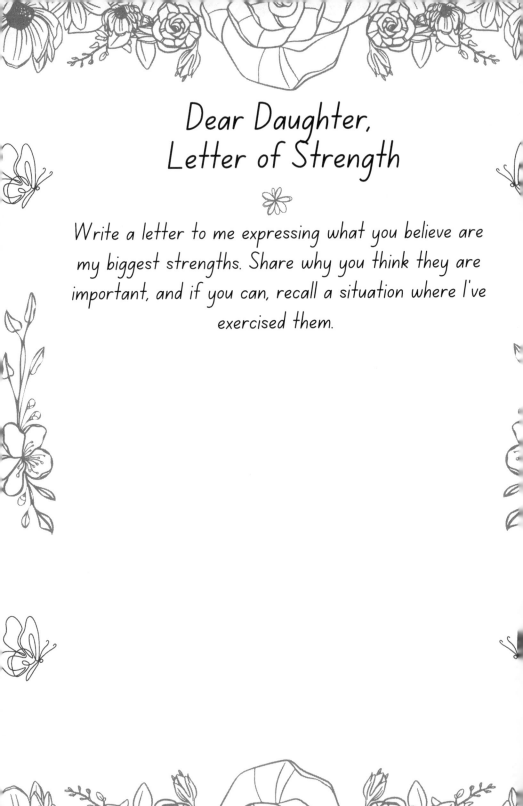

Write a letter to me expressing what you believe are my biggest strengths. Share why you think they are important, and if you can, recall a situation where I've exercised them.

Dear Mom,
Letter of Strength

Write a letter to me expressing what you believe are my biggest strengths. Share why you think they are important, and if you can, recall a situation where I've exercised them.

Dear Mom and Daughter, Letter of Family Love

Together write a letter to your whole family and express what you love about each member. Express love, gratitude, and appreciation.

Dear Daughter,
Nothing Left Unsaid...

On this page, write anything that you might have wanted to say but didn't get the chance to during this chapter with our Letters.

Dear Mom,
Nothing Left Unsaid...

On this page, write anything that you might have wanted to say but didn't get the chance to during this chapter with our Letters.

Chapter III
Memories and Milestones

The third chapter focuses on your joint memories and successfully finished milestones, as individuals, as mother and daughter, and as a family.

Families come in all shapes and sizes, and what unifies them all is the time and effort they have spent together. The things that we do together are the things that will forever tie us together. And this is exactly what makes a family.

What makes your family special? Where is everyone's place in the family tapestry? What makes you all unique? What sets you apart? In this chapter, you will have a chance to explore and have fun with exactly that.

Dear Daughter,
Special Family Moments

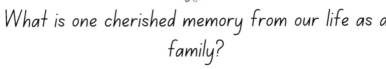

What is one cherished memory from our life as a family?

Draw the scene you remember most vividly.

Title this experience.

Dear Mom,
Special Family Moments

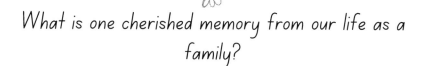

What is one cherished memory from our life as a family?

Draw the scene you remember most vividly.

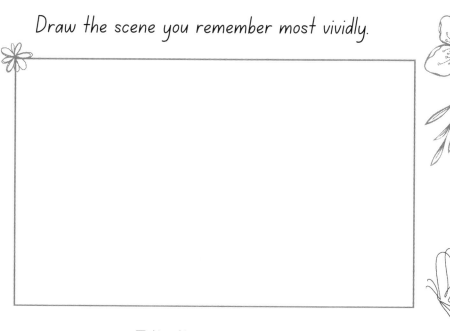

Title this experience.

Dear Mom and Daughter, Who's the best at...

Communicate, debate, and vote who in your family is the best in these areas:

Sports

Finding things

Making up stories

Driving

Cooking

Chatting

Dancing

Winning games

Organizing stuff

Singing

Dear Daughter,
Funny Mishaps

What are some of the funniest memories you have of our family?

Dear Mom,
Funny Mishaps

✳

What are some of the funniest memories you have of our family?

Dear Daughter,
Being Part of This

❊

What has been the most exciting part of being my child?

What am I pretty good at as a parent?

Dear Mom,
Being Part of This

✻

What has been the most exciting part of being my
parent?

What am I pretty good at as a child?

Dear Daughter,
Our Words

Brainstorm words that remind you of our family and house.

*Once both of you are done, compare the words and see if you have any matching ones or ones that are contradictory. You can develop this into a discussion.

Dear Mom,
Our Words

Brainstorm words that remind you of our family and house.

*Once both of you are done, compare the words and see if you have any matching ones or ones that are contradictory. You can develop this into a discussion.

Dear Daughter,
Nothing Left Unsaid...

On this page, write anything that you might have wanted to say but didn't get the chance to during this chapter about our Memories.

Dear Mom,
Nothing Left Unsaid...

On this page, write anything that you might have wanted to say but didn't get the chance to during this chapter about our Memories.

Chapter IV
Dreaming Together

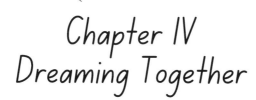

The fourth chapter of this journal is all about the future and the countless possibilities out there.

Through questions, prompts, and drawing exercises you can "peek" into what you hope your future will be and share it with the most important people around you.

You will be able to reevaluate and examine your expectations of yourself and others, as well as hear others' expectations of you. Then, you can talk and share with compassion and come up with ways to get and give support for the best future possible.

Dear Daughter,
Your future

❀

Make a list of what you want to achieve in the next 5 years.

....

....

....

....

....

....

Choose one thing that I can help you with and explain in more detail how I can do that.

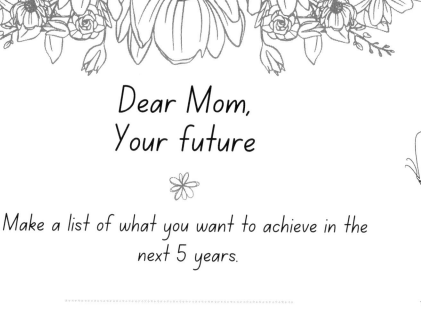

Dear Mom,
Your future

Make a list of what you want to achieve in the next 5 years.

....

....

....

....

....

....

Choose one thing that I can help you with and explain in more detail how I can do that.

Dear Mom and Daughter, Our Vision Board

Create a vision board for the future of your family. This can include pictures, drawings, positive affirmations, and quotes that reflect your family, values, visions for the future, vacations, things you want to achieve, or anything else you wish.

*Use old newspapers and magazines and cut pictures out of them to use them for the board.

Dear Daughter,
Family Bucket List

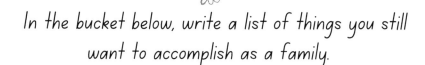

In the bucket below, write a list of things you still want to accomplish as a family.

*Cross-check your wishes for matching ones and develop a discussion about the most important things.

Dear Mom,
Family Bucket List

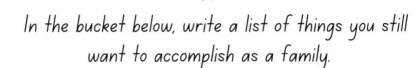

In the bucket below, write a list of things you still
want to accomplish as a family.

*Cross-check your wishes for matching ones and
develop a discussion about the most important things.

Dear Daughter,
Dreaming Jar

In the jar below, write what you want your mother to accomplish. They can be big and small, realistic or not-that-much. This is more about envisioning the full potential, not about real-life expectations.

Then, share them with your mom and see her reaction.

Dear Mom,
Dreaming Jar

In the jar below, write what you want your daughter to accomplish. They can be big and small, realistic or not-that-much. This is more about envisioning the full potential, not about real-life expectations.

Then, share them with your daughter and see her reaction.

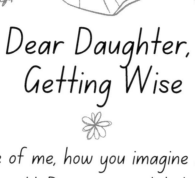

Dear Daughter,
Getting Wise

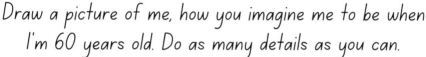

Draw a picture of me, how you imagine me to be when I'm 60 years old. Do as many details as you can.

Now, write 5 personality traits that you think I'll have then.

Dear Mom,
Getting Wise

Draw a picture of me, how you imagine me to be when
I'm 60 years old. Do as many details as you can.

Now, write 5 personality traits that you think
I'll have then.

Dear Daughter,
Nothing Left Unsaid...

On this page, write anything that you might have wanted to say but didn't get the chance to during this chapter about our Dreams.

Dear Mom,
Nothing Left Unsaid...

On this page, write anything that you might have wanted to say but didn't get the chance to during this chapter about our Dreams.

Chapter V
Heart-to-heart Conversations

Honesty is a virtue! And so is compassion. The fifth chapter of this journal is all about honest, intimate conversations about what is important to each of you.

On the next pages, you two will get the chance to talk about your most important beliefs, values, life lessons, hardships, and accomplishments.

Teach and learn, talk and listen. These conversations are about what is important in life, and they can be a fortified foundation for your unlimited love and respect for each other.

Dear Daughter,
Inspirational Quotes

Share your favorite quotes and why they inspire you.

Dear Mom,
Inspirational Quotes

Share your favorite quotes and why they inspire you.

Dear Mom and Daughter, Values to live by

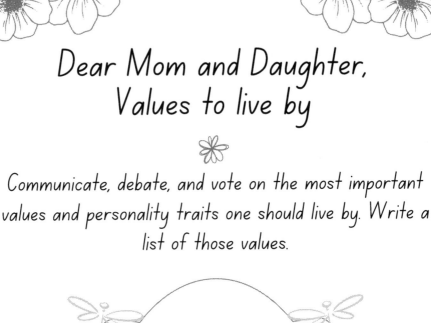

Communicate, debate, and vote on the most important values and personality traits one should live by. Write a list of those values.

Dear Daughter,
Give some, Get some

❀

What is one of your proudest accomplishments?
How did you achieve that thing?

What did you sacrifice to achieve that?

Do you believe that I (and our family) see, acknowledge,
and appreciate that accomplishment of yours? What
can we do to show greater appreciation?

Dear Mom,
Give some, Get some

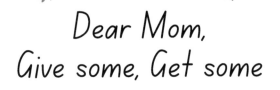

What is one of your proudest accomplishments?
How did you achieve that thing?

What did you sacrifice to achieve that?

Do you believe that I (and our family) see, acknowledge,
and appreciate that accomplishment of yours? What
can we do to show greater appreciation?

Dear Daughter,
Switching Roles

Write a short story about how you believe my regular day goes. Try to put yourself into my shoes and see what is good and what is difficult about my day.

After you are both done, share the stories with each other.

Dear Mom,
Switching Roles

Write a short story about how you believe my regular day goes. Try to put yourself into my shoes and see what is good and what is difficult about my day.

After you are both done, share the stories with each other.

Dear Daughter,
Life Lessons

Write about a life lesson you've learned from me.
How has this lesson shaped you?

Dear Mom,
Life Lessons

✳

Write about a life lesson you've learned from me.
How has this lesson shaped you?

Dear Daughter,
Nothing Left Unsaid...

On this page, write anything that you might have wanted to say but didn't get the chance to during this chapter about our Heart Conversations.

Dear Mom,
Nothing Left Unsaid...

On this page, write anything that you might have wanted to say but didn't get the chance to during this chapter about Heart Conversations.

Chapter VI
Creative Expression

The sixth chapter of this journal will get you hands-on on creating art and creatively expressing yourselves.

Being creative or making art is not about coming up with the next "Mona Lisa." It's about exploring your creativity and expression through different techniques.

In this chapter, you will get the chance to free yourself from rules and expectations and just creatively and spontaneously express yourself. Don't strive to make it perfect, strive to make it uniquely yours!

Dear Daughter,
Proud of Me

When have I made you most proud of me?

Draw how you remember that experience.

Dear Mom,
Proud of Me

When have I made you most proud of me?

Draw how you remember that experience.

Dear Daughter,
My Happy Place

Draw a picture of the most relaxing place you can imagine. Don't restrict yourself - it can be a real-life place, an imaginary one, indoor, outdoor, or anything else.

Then, share it with your mom and explain why this place relaxes you.

Dear Mom,
My Happy Place

❀

Draw a picture of the most relaxing place you can imagine. Don't restrict yourself - it can be a real-life place, an imaginary one, indoor, outdoor, or anything else.

Then, share it with your daughter and explain why this place relaxes you.

Dear Daughter,
I see You, You see Me

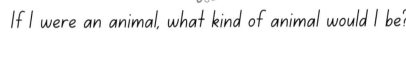

If I were an animal, what kind of animal would I be?

Draw a picture.

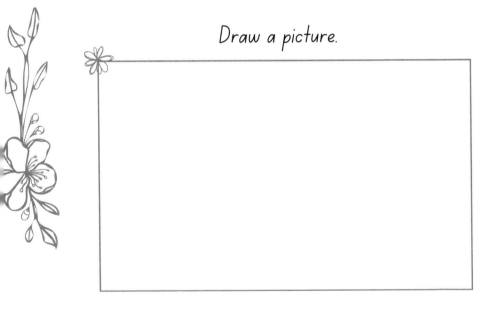

Why did you choose this animal? Which of my
personality traits remind you of this animal?

Dear Mom,
I see You, You see Me

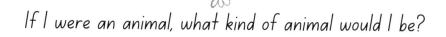

If I were an animal, what kind of animal would I be?

Draw a picture.

Why did you choose this animal? Which of my
personality traits remind you of this animal?

Dear Mom and Daughter, Our Fairytale

Write a fairytale together. Come up with a main character, a challenge that the character has to overcome, and a creative way to achieve it.

Dear Mom and Daughter, Our Poetry

Write a song together that will reflect the importance of mother and daughter relationship and love.
Have one of you start and write the first verse, and then the other continue the next verse. Repeat the process until you have a song.

Dear Daughter,
Nothing Left Unsaid...

On this page, write anything that you might have wanted to say but didn't get the chance to during this chapter about our Creative Expression.

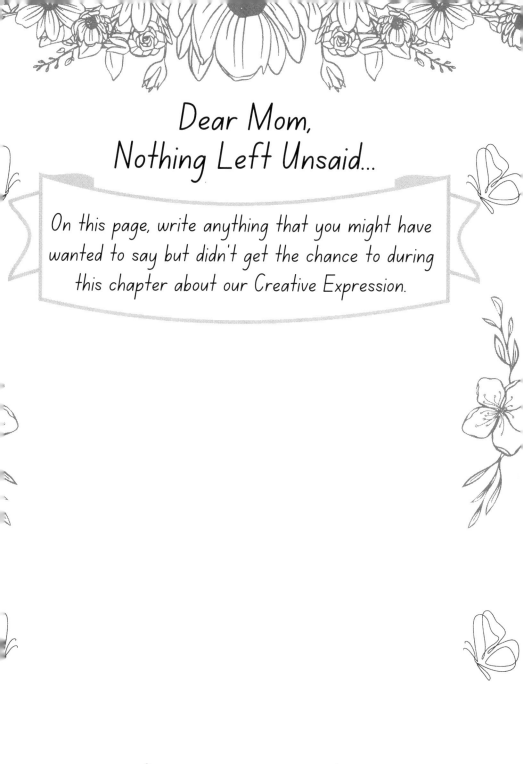

Dear Mom,
Nothing Left Unsaid...

On this page, write anything that you might have wanted to say but didn't get the chance to during this chapter about our Creative Expression.

Chapter VII
Cooking and Baking Memories

In this chapter, it's time to share a little knowledge and a little love connected to food!

Cooking is one of the main ways in which we connect and show each other our love and appreciation. So, during this chapter, you'll have the chance to talk about your favorite recipes and share some of your cooking wisdom.

This chapter will also give you space to do some cooking lists and food traditions, allowing you to have a ready go-to place any time you get stuck on "What's for dinner?" or "What should we cook for this occasion?"
Keep your tummies as full as your hearts!

Dear Daughter,
My Favorite Meal

Write down the recipe of your favorite main course
meal and the step-by-step process of making it.

Ingredients:

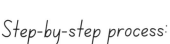

Step-by-step process:

Dear Mom,
My Favorite Meal

Write down the recipe of your favorite main course meal and the step-by-step process of making it.

Ingredients:

_____   _____

_____   _____

_____   _____

_____   _____

_____

Step-by-step process:

Dear Mom and Daughter,
Our Favorite Recipe

Communicate, debate, and vote and find one main course dish that you both love. Write down the step-by-step process of making it.

Ingredients:

Step-by-step process:

Dear Daughter,
My Favorite Sweet

Write down the recipe of your favorite sweet/cake and the step-by-step process of making it.

Ingredients:

Step-by-step process:

Dear Mom,
My Favorite Sweet

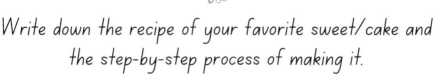

Write down the recipe of your favorite sweet/cake and
the step-by-step process of making it.

Ingredients:

Step-by-step process:

Dear Mom and Daughter,
Our Favorite Bake

Communicate, debate, and vote and find one sweet/cake
that you both love. Write down the step-by-step
process of making it.

Ingredients:

_____   _____
_____   _____
_____   _____
_____   _____
_____   _____
_____

Step-by-step process:

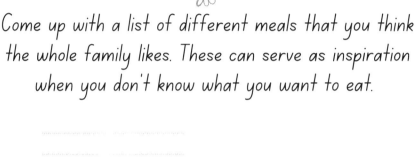

Dear Daughter,
What do we eat?

Come up with a list of different meals that you think the whole family likes. These can serve as inspiration when you don't know what you want to eat.

Communicate and see if you both have similar or the same dishes mentioned.

Dear Mom,
What do we eat?

Come up with a list of different meals that you think the whole family likes. These can serve as inspiration when you don't know what you want to eat.

Communicate and see if you both have similar or the same dishes mentioned.

Dear Mom and Daughter, Go-to Foods

Write a list of the foods that you, as a family, most often have on different occasions.

Picnic foods

Movie night foods

Birthday foods

Dear Mom and Daughter, Food Traditions

Think about and write a list of the food traditions that you as a family have on certain holidays and special occasions (like birthday foods, religious holidays, small family celebrations). Don't forget to name the traditions at the top, like on the previous page!

Dear Daughter,
Nothing Left Unsaid...

On this page, write anything that you might have wanted to say but didn't get the chance to during this chapter about our Cooking and Baking.

Dear Mom,
Nothing Left Unsaid...

On this page, write anything that you might have wanted to say but didn't get the chance to during this chapter about our Cooking and Baking.

Chapter VIII
Book and Movie Clubs

In this chapter, you will get the chance to make your own book and movie clubs and talk about the art that has inspired you.

Aside from being quite fun and entertaining, books and movies can be very educational and thought-provoking. They can also be very inspiring, bring forth intense emotions or get you to sympathize with people completely different from you.

Through different questions and lists in this chapter, you can share with each other the most inspiring books that you've read and movies that you've seen, as well as give recommendations and open discussions.

Dear Daughter,
Favorite Books List

Write a list of the most memorable books you've read.

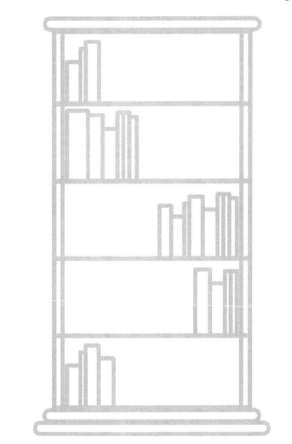

Go over the book list and rate them 1 to 5, with no.1 being your favorite book.

Dear Mom,
Favorite Books List

Write a list of the most memorable books you've read.

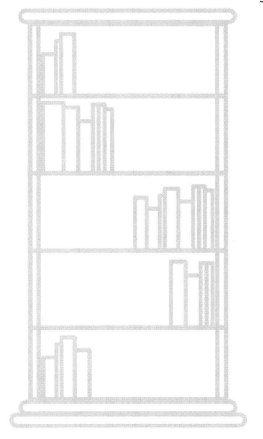

Go over the book list and rate them 1 to 5, with no.1 being your favorite book.

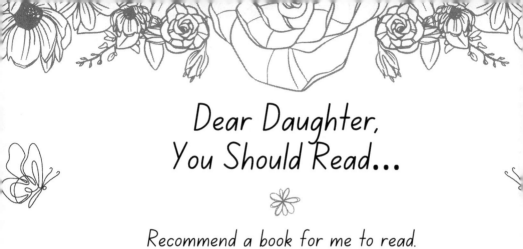

Dear Daughter,
You Should Read...

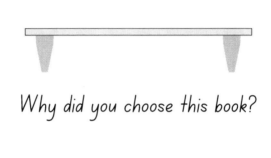

Recommend a book for me to read.

Why did you choose this book?

What is your favorite part from it?

Dear Mom,
You Should Read...

Recommend a book for me to read.

Why did you choose this book?

What is your favorite part from it?

Dear Daughter,
Favorite Movie

What is your favorite movie?

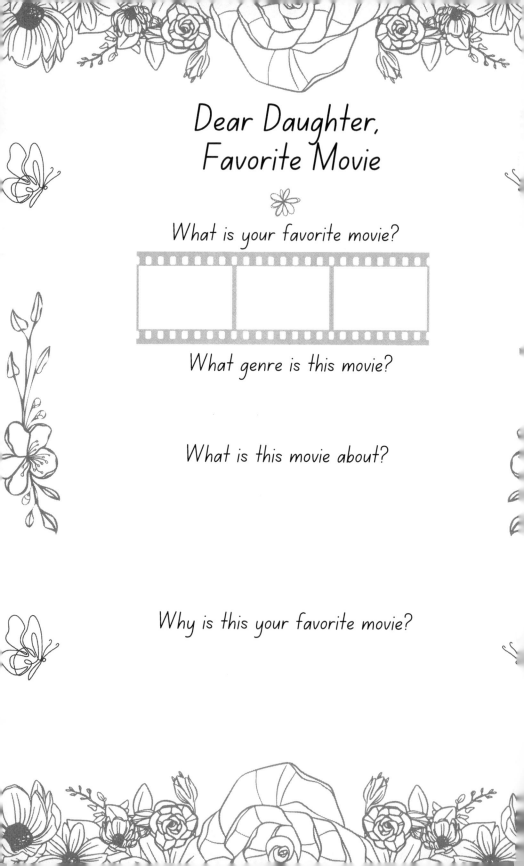

What genre is this movie?

What is this movie about?

Why is this your favorite movie?

Dear Mom,
Favorite Movie

What is your favorite movie?

What genre is this movie?

What is this movie about?

Why is this your favorite movie?

Dear Daughter,
You Should Watch...

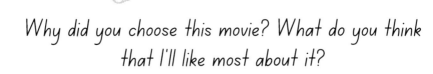

Recommend a movie for me to see.

Why did you choose this movie? What do you think
that I'll like most about it?

What is your favorite scene from it?

Dear Mom,
You Should Watch...

Recommend a movie for me to see.

Why did you choose this movie? What do you think that I'll like most about it?

What is your favorite scene from it?

Dear Mom and Daughter,
A Movie We've Seen Together

Communicate and rate movies to find a movie that you both watched and liked.
Together, draw a picture of your favorite scene from that movie.

Dear Daughter,
Nothing Left Unsaid...

On this page, write anything that you might have wanted to say but didn't get the chance to during this chapter about our Books and Movies.

Dear Mom,
Nothing Left Unsaid...

On this page, write anything that you might have wanted to say but didn't get the chance to during this chapter about our Books and Movies.

Chapter IX
Travel and Adventure

The fun, entertaining, and one-of-a-kind experiences we have in life are the things that matter in the end. One such thing is traveling and the adventures weaved through them.

In this chapter, you will have the chance to recall some of the most interesting travels and adventures you've had together and alone. You will share some of the most memorable experiences and envision what you would like to do in the future.

This one's for the road, so have fun!

Dear Daughter,
Cherished Memory of a Family Trip

What is your favorite family trip that we've had?

What do you remember most vividly about that trip?

Draw the most memorable memory from that trip.

Dear Mom,
Cherished Memory of a Family Trip

What is your favorite family trip that we've had?

What do you remember most vividly about that trip?

Draw the most memorable memory from that trip.

Dear Daughter,
Cherished Memory of a Solo Trip

Describe the most memorable trip you have been on,
on your own, or with friends.

Paint a picture of the scene you remember most vividly
from that trip.

Dear Mom,
Cherished Memory of a Solo Trip

Describe the most memorable trip you have been on, on your own, or with friends.

Paint a picture of the scene you remember most vividly from that trip.

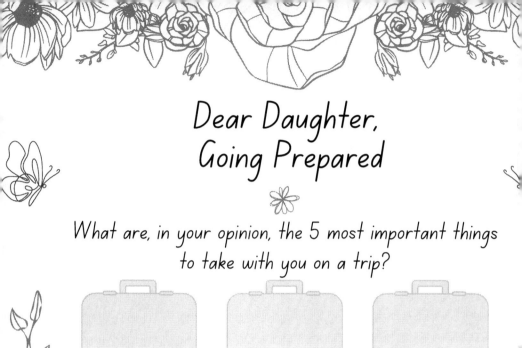

Dear Daughter,
Going Prepared

What are, in your opinion, the 5 most important things
to take with you on a trip?

Share with me 4 traveling tips you deem essential.

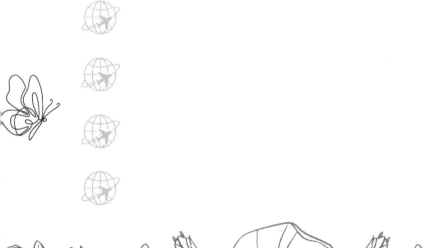

Dear Mom,
Going Prepared

What are, in your opinion, the 5 most important things
to take with you on a trip?

Share with me 4 traveling tips you deem essential.

Dear Daughter,
The Perfect Vacation

What would be the best vacation for us two to go on?

What activities would we do together?

Draw a scene from that vacation.

Dear Mom,
The Perfect Vacation

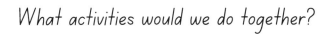

What would be the best vacation for us two to go on?

What activities would we do together?

Draw a scene from that vacation.

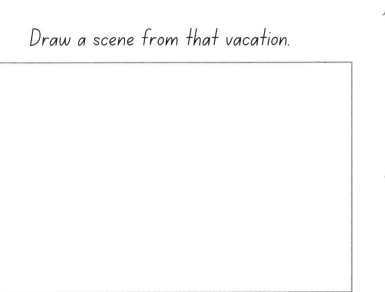

Dear Daughter,
Nothing Left Unsaid...

On this page, write anything that you might have wanted to say but didn't get the chance to during this chapter about our Travels and Adventures.

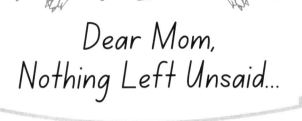

Dear Mom,
Nothing Left Unsaid...

On this page, write anything that you might have wanted to say but didn't get the chance to during this chapter about our Travels and Adventures.

Chapter X
Health and Wellness Journey

Taking care of yourself is the prerequisite for taking care of others. Self-health and self-care are essential parts of life, and the more we do them, the easier it is to maintain them as habits.

Through this chapter, you will get the chance to share some of your health, wellness, and beauty secrets, routines, wishes, and goals.

Everything is better when you have someone to do it with, so, you will also be able to motivate each other and plan joint healthy activities.
Stay healthy together!

Dear Daughter,
Living Healthy

What are 5 healthy life tips you would give to me?

What are 3 healthy foods you like?

What are 3 healthy drinks you like?

Dear Mom,
Living Healthy

❀

What are 5 healthy life tips you would give to me?

What are 3 healthy foods you like?

What are 3 healthy drinks you like?

Dear Daughter,
Self-Care

How do you express love to yourself?

What is your evening self-care routine?

What are 3 activities that you love to do to relax and destress?

Dear Mom,
Self-Care

How do you express love to yourself?

What is your evening self-care routine?

What are 3 activities that you love to do to relax and destress?

Dear Daughter,
Joint Wellness

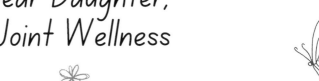

Come up with a wellness activity you would like us to do together.

Draw the activity below.

Explain how we would benefit from it and try to organize a time when we can do it.

Dear Mom,
Joint Wellness

Come up with a wellness activity you would like us to do together.

Draw the activity below.

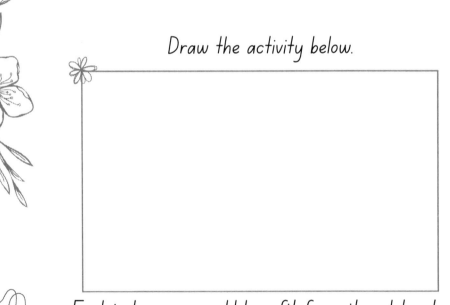

Explain how we would benefit from it and try to organize a time when we can do it.

Dear Mom and Daughter, Our Motivation Page

Together, come up with positive affirmations and motivational quotes that will keep you motivated to practice health and wellness activities.

*Go back to this page when you need motivation.

Dear Daughter,
How Can I Help?

Is there something from your health and wellness journey that I can help with?

How exactly do you want me to help you with it?

What would this help mean to you? Why is it important?

Dear Mom,
How Can I Help?

✿

Is there something from your health and wellness journey that I can help with?

How exactly do you want me to help you with it?

What would this help mean to you? Why is it important?

Dear Daughter,
Nothing Left Unsaid...

On this page, write anything that you might have wanted to say but didn't get the chance to during this chapter about our Health and Wellness.

Dear Mom,
Nothing Left Unsaid...

On this page, write anything that you might have wanted to say but didn't get the chance to during this chapter about our Health and Wellness.

Chapter XI
Lessons Learned, Wisdom Shared

Learning from each other is a wonderful way of sharing wisdom with those important to us and learning without having to make mistakes on our own.

Through different exercises, questions, and activities, this chapter of the journal will do exactly that - prompt you to share some lessons learned and some wisdom gained.

In this chapter, you will do so by talking about your life challenges and problems, as well as the things you did to overcome them. This conversation will inevitably lead to expressing your power, as well as providing support and motivation to the other.

Dear Daughter,
Challenges are Teachers

✳

Write about one big challenge that you have faced and how you overcame it.

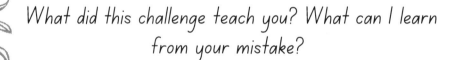

What did this challenge teach you? What can I learn from your mistake?

Dear Mom,
Challenges are Teachers

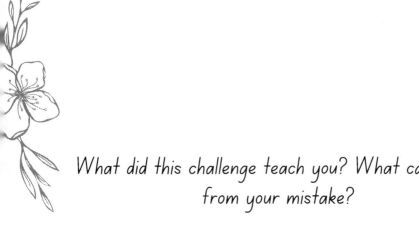

Write about one big challenge that you have faced and how you overcame it.

What did this challenge teach you? What can I learn from your mistake?

Dear Daughter,
My Power

❀

What is your biggest strength?

Have you consciously worked on it to make it your strength, or did it just happen?

Do you think I notice and appreciate your strength?

Dear Mom,
My Power

What is your biggest strength?

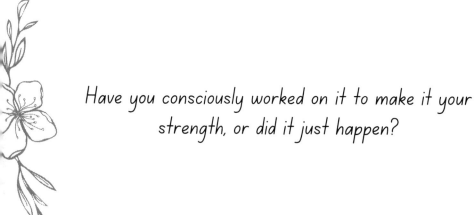

Have you consciously worked on it to make it your strength, or did it just happen?

Do you think I notice and appreciate your strength?

Dear Daughter,
Wanting the Best for You

❋

Write a list of advice you think that I'll benefit from.
They can be connected to particular life areas or broad
things about life.

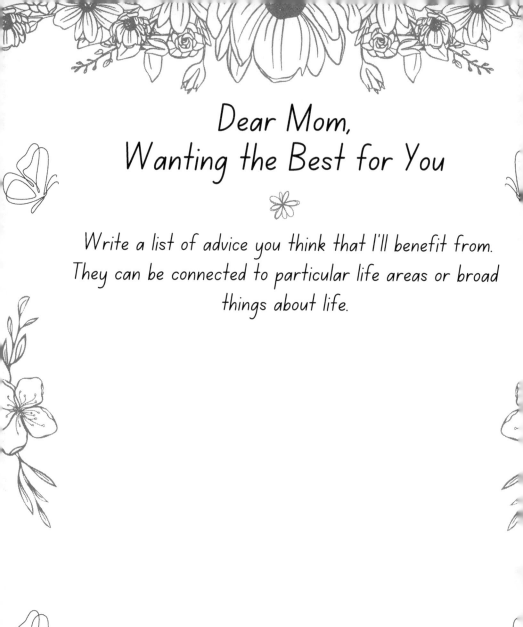

Dear Mom,
Wanting the Best for You

✳

Write a list of advice you think that I'll benefit from.
They can be connected to particular life areas or broad
things about life.

Dear Daughter,
Understanding You

❋

What is one thing you wish I understood better about you?

Where do you think my misunderstanding comes from?

What do you need to feel more understood?

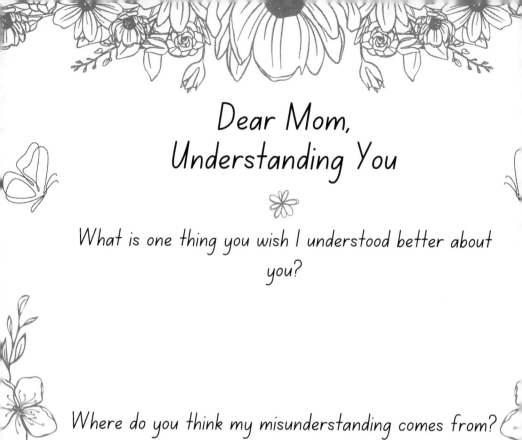

Dear Mom,
Understanding You

What is one thing you wish I understood better about you?

Where do you think my misunderstanding comes from?

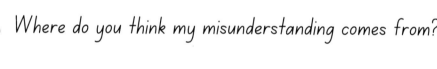

What do you need to feel more understood?

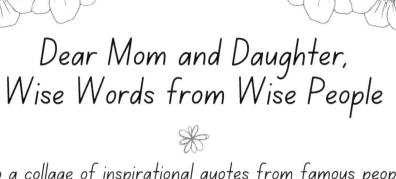

Dear Mom and Daughter,
Wise Words from Wise People

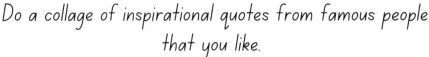

Do a collage of inspirational quotes from famous people that you like.

*Feel free to use magazines, newspapers, or internet research.

Dear Daughter,
Nothing Left Unsaid...

On this page, write anything that you might have wanted to say but didn't get the chance to during this chapter about our Lessons and Wisdom.

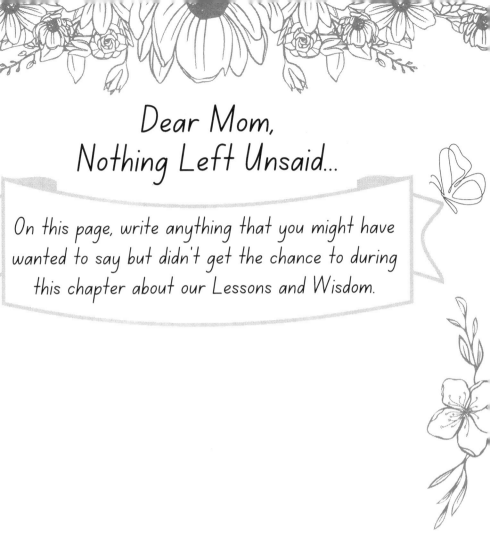

Dear Mom,
Nothing Left Unsaid...

On this page, write anything that you might have wanted to say but didn't get the chance to during this chapter about our Lessons and Wisdom.

Chapter XII
Gratitude and Love

Even though we truly and deeply know in our hearts that we love and appreciate the people around us, we should often share that with those around us and acknowledge all their efforts toward us.

In this last chapter of our journal, we will focus on showing positive emotions of love, appreciation, understanding, and care for the other person.

The exercises in this chapter will ask you to think about and express your positive emotions toward the people around you, as well as hear words of appreciation and acts of love from them.

Dear Daughter,
A Day to be Grateful for

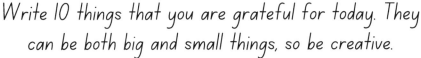

Write 10 things that you are grateful for today. They can be both big and small things, so be creative.

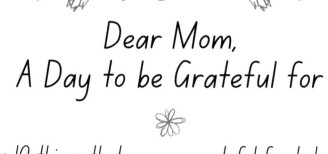

Dear Mom,
A Day to be Grateful for

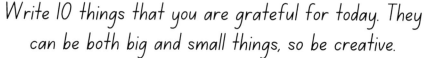

Write 10 things that you are grateful for today. They can be both big and small things, so be creative.

Dear Daughter,
Ideal Words of Appreciation

What would you like to hear from me to feel loved and appreciated?

What words of appreciation or gratitude can I use when I want to thank you?

In what ways can I express my love for you, so you feel loved and appreciated?

Dear Mom,
Ideal Words of Appreciation

What would you like to hear from me to feel loved and appreciated?

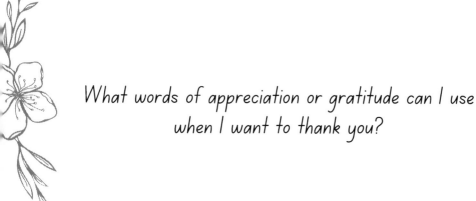

What words of appreciation or gratitude can I use when I want to thank you?

In what ways can I express my love for you, so you feel loved and appreciated?

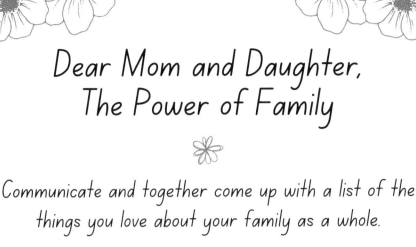

Dear Mom and Daughter,
The Power of Family

Communicate and together come up with a list of the things you love about your family as a whole.

Dear Daughter,
To Feel Loved

❀

What do you need to feel loved by me?

What words of affirmation could I say to you to make you feel better when you're down?

What gifts can I give you to brighten your day?

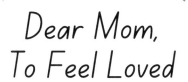

Dear Mom,
To Feel Loved

What do you need to feel loved by me?

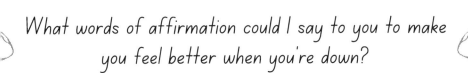

What words of affirmation could I say to you to make you feel better when you're down?

What gifts can I give you to brighten your day?

Dear Daughter,
Nothing Left Unsaid...

On this page, write anything that you might have wanted to say but didn't get the chance to during this chapter about our Gratitude and Love.

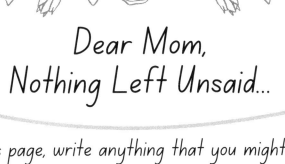

Dear Mom,
Nothing Left Unsaid...

On this page, write anything that you might have wanted to say but didn't get the chance to during this chapter about our Gratitude and Love.

Ending Reflections

Unfortunately, we are coming close to the end of the journal.

Now, it's time to add your uniqueness to it by giving some last reflections, words of wisdom, and heartfelt emotions about the whole journey and the time you spent together filling it out, drawing in it, talking about it, recalling, and commenting.

In this chapter, it's time for all of us to say goodbye and share how we feel. But, don't feel sad for reaching the end - this journal is a keepsake for years to come. It will stay with you forever and you can always go down memory lane through it.

Dear Daughter,
Thank you note from you

Write a short gratitude note about this experience.
Write about the emotions you had as you were jointly
doing this journal and how you feel now once you have
finished it.

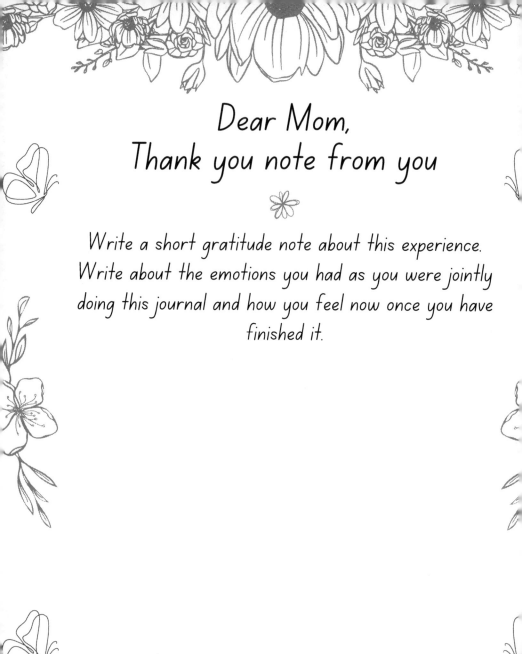

Dear Mom,
Thank you note from you

Write a short gratitude note about this experience. Write about the emotions you had as you were jointly doing this journal and how you feel now once you have finished it.

Thank You Note
from the Author

We've come to the last page of this journal. With my questions and exercises, I feel like a silent fellow traveler with you two! It's been a pleasure to be able to be part of your journey.

Now, all that's left is to thank you for the dedication and your willingness to share and explore your own, and the individuality of the other. To be open to listening to new and old things, to share your thoughts and emotions, to express yourself and your uniqueness.

It is my pleasure to have given you something that will testify to your irreplaceable connection as a mother and daughter, and serve as a shining beacon that crowns your relationship.

With Love,
The Author

Made in the USA
Coppell, TX
15 November 2024

40315480R00083

This "Threads of Love: Mother-Daughter Journal" is a life-long keepsake and a testament to your irreplaceable connection.

Through different activities, questions, and instructions, you two will weave together your memories and dreams and have heartfelt conversations that will strengthen your threads of love.

Besides spending a wonderful time together filling out the content, the journal will be a precious testament to your connection for years to come, allowing you to go down memory lane whenever you wish.

ISBN 9798339659228

9000

9 798339 659228